On Memory and Reminiscence

The Science of Memory and Thought

A Modern Translation

Adapted for the Contemporary Reader

Aristotle

Translated by Tim Zengerink

Table of Contents

Preface: Message to the Reader. iv

Introduction. .1

On Memory and Reminiscence. 10

PREFACE

MESSAGE TO THE READER

Dear Reader,

Thank you for choosing this edition; it is more than just a book—you are reading a living thread of humanity's literary heritage.

We'd like to invite you to **gain immediate, unlimited digital & audiobook access** to hundreds of the most treasured literary classics ever written—along with the option to **secure deluxe paperback, hardcover & box set editions at printing cost**. Together, we can **spark a new global literary renaissance** alongside our small, independent publishing house called "The Library of Alexandria."

Thousands of years ago, the Library of Alexandria stood as a beacon of knowledge—until it was lost to history. We aim to reignite that spirit of preservation and discovery right now, in the modern age—only this time, it's accessible to all, in every language and every format.

Picture a world where every timeless classic, novel, poem, or philosophical treatise is not only available to read but also updated for today's readers—modernized, translated into any language or dialect, and ready to enjoy in any format you choose, whether that is in an eBook, audiobook, paperback, or deluxe hardcover & box set version a printing cost.

By joining our movement to **rebuild the modern Library of Alexandria**, you become part of an unprecedented mission to offer:

- **Unlimited Audiobook & eBook Access to the Greatest Classics of All Time**

  Instantly explore thousands of legendary works, from Plato and Shakespeare to Jane Austen and Leo Tolstoy. All are instantly ready to read or listen to, giving you a complete literary universe at your fingertips.

- **Paperback & Deluxe Editions at Printing Costs:**

  Purchase any title in a paperback, deluxe hardbound, or deluxe boxset edition at printing costs, shipped right to your doorstep. Curate your personal library of Alexandria with editions worthy of display—crafted to last, designed to captivate, and delivered straight to your door.

- **Modern translations for Contemporary Readers in all languages and dialects**

  Discover a vast selection of classics reimagined in clear, current language—no more struggling with outdated phrases or obscure references. Next to the original versions, we aim to offer translations in as many languages and dialects as possible.

As we continue our translation efforts and add new languages, readers everywhere can connect with these works as if they were written today. *By bridging linguistic divides, you're contributing to ensuring that these timeless stories become more meaningful, accessible, and inspiring for people across the globe.*

- **Your Personal Library of Alexandria:**

  Over the months and years, you'll curate a unique physical archive of classics—each volume a testament to your taste, curiosity, and love of knowledge. It's not just about owning books—it's about curating a cultural legacy you'll cherish and pass down for generations to come.

- **Join a Global Literary Renaissance:**

  Your support fuels an ongoing mission: allowing us to reinvest in offering deluxe print editions (including special boxsets) at their true cost, broaden the range of available formats and translations, and extend the reach of these works to new audiences worldwide. By joining today, you're not just preserving a legacy of masterpieces; *you set in motion a powerful wave of literary accessibility.*

We are more than a publisher—we're a movement, and we can't do it alone. Your support lets us scale our mission, preserving and reimagining history's greatest works for tomorrow's readers.

Become a Torchbearer of knowledge.

Thank you for picking up this book and allowing us into your literary journey. As you turn the pages, know that you're part of something larger: a global effort to keep these stories alive, share their wisdom across borders and generations, and spark a true cultural revival for the modern era.

If this resonates with you—please consider taking the next step. By visiting:
www.libraryofalexandria.com

With gratitude and a shared love of knowledge,

The Modern Library of Alexandria Team

Visit:

www.libraryofalexandria.com

Or scan the code below:

Introduction

A ncient Greece was a civilization famous for its great contributions to philosophy, politics, art, and science. It thrived from the 8th century BCE until the Roman Empire started to decline. Greece's city-states, especially Athens, were the heart of culture and intellectual thought. This was the time when democracy began, impressive buildings like the Parthenon were built, and famous playwrights like Sophocles and Euripides produced their works. The Greeks' curiosity about the world around them laid the foundation for Western philosophy. Thinkers like Socrates, Plato, and later Aristotle, pushed the limits of what people understood about the world.

Greek society was deeply connected to theism, which focused on a large group of gods and goddesses who were believed to control every part of life. But this system did not prevent people from exploring new ideas. In fact, it coexisted with a growing interest in finding logical explanations for nature and human life. Intellectuals would often debate and discuss these ideas in public places like the Agora. Aristotle grew up in this dynamic environment, learning from earlier philosophers, and later challenging and expanding their ideas.

Aristotle's Life

Aristotle was born in 384 BCE in a small town called Stagira, located in northern Greece. His father, Nicomachus, was a doctor for King Amyntas of Macedon, and this allowed Aristotle to be around the Macedonian royal court from a young age. When his parents passed away, Aristotle was sent to Athens at the age of 17 to pursue his education. Athens was the center of intellectual life in Greece, and Aristotle joined Plato's Academy, which was the most respected school of the time. The Academy was a place where students discussed everything from ethics to science. Although Aristotle learned a lot from Plato, he did not always agree with him, especially when it came to metaphysics, which deals with the nature of reality.

After spending almost 20 years at the Academy, Aristotle left Athens around 347 BCE after Plato's death. He traveled around different cities in Greece, continuing to study and learn. In 343 BCE, he was invited to the court of King Philip II of Macedon, where he became the tutor of Philip's son, Alexander, who would later become known as Alexander the Great. Aristotle taught Alexander about philosophy, ethics, politics, and science. Aristotle's influence is visible in Alexander's leadership style, which showed respect for knowledge and strategic thinking.

After teaching Alexander, Aristotle returned to Athens in 335 BCE, where he opened his own school called the Lyceum. Unlike Plato's Academy, the Lyceum focused more on recording knowledge and observing nature. Aristotle and his students performed research, studied animals, and took notes on what they observed. The Lyceum became a major center of learning, and it rivaled Plato's Academy. This is also where Aristotle wrote many of his famous works.

Later in life, after the death of Alexander in 323 BCE, the political climate in Athens became difficult for Aristotle because of his connections to the Macedonian court. Accused of disrespecting the gods, Aristotle decided to leave Athens. He fled to Chalcis, where he passed away in 322 BCE. Even though he had to leave Athens, his legacy lived on through his many writings and the influence of his school, the Lyceum.

Aristotle's Impact on Western Thought

No figure looms larger over the development of Western philosophy and science than Aristotle. A student of Plato and tutor to Alexander the Great, he unified logic, ethics, politics, rhetoric, and metaphysics into a coherent system that shaped intellectual inquiry for centuries. Although his writings reflect the best knowledge of his era, they also reveal a distinctive way of understanding the world—one that balances observation with rigorous logical analysis. Over time, this method has profoundly influenced everything from political theory to modern scientific methodology.

Aristotle approached knowledge as an interconnected whole, seeing each field of study as a vital path toward truth. While many earlier thinkers focused on abstract concepts, he emphasized direct observation of the natural world. By systematically examining and classifying what he saw, Aristotle laid the groundwork for the empirical methods now central to modern science. Although our understanding of nature has evolved, his legacy endures in today's emphasis on evidence-based research.

Logic: The Foundation of Rational Inquiry

Often hailed as the "father of formal logic," Aristotle introduced a system of reasoning that shaped intellectual discourse for over two millennia. In works like the Organon, he analyzed how valid conclusions are drawn from premises and introduced syllogisms—deductive arguments that became standard tools in philosophy, theology, and science. Even contemporary logic, despite its modern mathematical and symbolic advancements, can trace many of its core principles back to Aristotle's pioneering analyses.

Metaphysics: Exploring the Nature of Reality

Aristotle's Metaphysics offered one of the earliest comprehensive explorations of existence at its most fundamental level. There, he described the nature of "being qua being" and introduced the concepts of potentiality and actuality to explain how things change and develop. These ideas deeply influenced medieval scholastics—both Christian and Islamic—who integrated Aristotelian reasoning into their theological frameworks. Today, discussions about consciousness, identity, and free will still reference these Aristotelian notions.

Ethics and the Pursuit of the Good Life

In the Nicomachean Ethics, Aristotle proposed that the ultimate aim of human life is eudaimonia, often translated as "happiness" or "flourishing." He argued that we achieve this through virtue, developed by cultivating good habits guided by reason. His famous Doctrine of the Mean asserts that moral virtue resides between two extremes—for instance, courage lies between recklessness and cowardice. This focus on character formation has profoundly shaped the tradition known as "virtue ethics," influencing modern debates on moral education, personal development, and what it means to live well.

Politics: The Role of the Individual in the City-State

Aristotle's practical approach to ethics naturally extended into political theory. In Politics, he explored various forms of government—monarchy, aristocracy, oligarchy, democracy—and weighed their merits and pitfalls. For Aristotle, a well-ordered polis (city-state) exists not merely for survival or trade but to enable its citizens to live virtuous, fulfilling lives. His conviction that ethics and politics are intertwined remains influential, informing contemporary discussions on citizenship, governance, and justice.

Rhetoric: The Art of Persuasion

In his treatise Rhetoric, Aristotle examined how persuasion works, detailing how arguments must appeal to ethos (credibility), pathos (emotion), and logos (logic). This clear framework for effective communication continues to guide public speakers, legal advocates, and writers. From ancient courtroom orations to modern political campaigns, Aristotelian rhetoric underpins many of the strategies people use to sway audiences and shape public opinion.

Beyond these core subjects, Aristotle made significant contributions to biology, physics, psychology, and aesthetics. In the Poetics, for example, he investigated why humans respond so powerfully to tragic drama, pioneering the concept of catharsis— the emotional release that audiences feel through art. Throughout the medieval period, thinkers like Thomas Aquinas integrated Aristotle's theories into Christian theology, while Islamic philosophers such as Avicenna and Averroes preserved, interpreted, and expanded upon his works.

Across centuries of reinterpretation and debate, Aristotle remains a living voice in contemporary thought. His insistence on systematically gathering evidence and connecting it to logical principles laid the foundation for what we now recognize as the scientific method. His inquiries into human flourishing, civic responsibility, and the nature of argument continue to spark discussion and inspire new research. From personal ethics to societal organization, Aristotle's ideas help us frame enduring questions about how best to live, learn, and understand reality.

In sum, Aristotle stands as a foundational pillar of Western thought. He bridged abstract theorizing and practical inquiry, bequeathing a vision of knowledge that values both reason and experience. From ethics and politics to science and art, his ideas have been woven into countless intellectual traditions. Even today, as we grapple with questions of morality, governance, and truth, we walk in the footsteps of an ancient thinker whose breadth of insight and depth of analysis continue to guide our pursuit of wisdom.

Final Thoughts

By preserving Aristotle's legacy, we protect the intellectual depth and rigor that defined his way of understanding the world. His systematic way of asking questions, his classification of knowledge, and his ethical theories are still relevant today, providing a model for critical thinking across many subjects. This preservation is important not just for philosophy students but for anyone interested in the foundations of human thought and the development of ideas that shape the world we live in.

One of the difficulties in studying Aristotle's work is that his ideas and language are complex. Translating these works into our modern language is a key step in making his profound insights easier for more people to understand. By putting his ideas into today's language, more readers can engage with his thoughts, even if they don't have a background in classical studies. Making Aristotle's work accessible means adapting them to modern ways of thinking without losing their original depth. This helps bridge the gap between ancient and modern readers, making sure Aristotle's work stays relevant.

On Memory and Reminiscence

Next, we need to talk about memory and remembering—what they are, what causes them, and which part of the soul they belong to, along with the process of recollecting. People who have a good memory are not always the same people who are good at recollecting. In fact, people who are slow thinkers tend to have a better memory, while those who are quick-witted and clever are better at recollecting.

First, we need to understand what memory is about, because this is where mistakes often happen. You can't remember the future; that's more a matter of opinion or expectation. Some people even believe there is a science of expectation, like divination. You also can't remember the present; this is something we only experience through our senses. By using our senses, we don't know the future or the past, only the present. But memory is always about the past. No one would say they remember something that's happening in the moment, like seeing a white object as they look at it. And you wouldn't say you remember something you are actively thinking about, like when you are studying or contemplating something right now. In these cases, you're simply perceiving or knowing it. But when someone knows something, and they aren't actively thinking about it, that's when they remember it. For example, you remember that the angles of a triangle add up to two right angles, or that you learned something before, or you heard or saw something before. Whenever you remember, you think to yourself, "I heard this before" or "I thought of this before."

So, memory is not the same as perception or understanding, but it is something that happens to one of these after some time has passed. As mentioned earlier, there is no such thing as remembering the present. The present is for perception, and the future is for expectation, but the past is what we remember. All memory, therefore, involves time passing. Only animals that can perceive time are capable of remembering, and the organ that helps them perceive time is also the one that helps them remember.

We've already discussed the idea of "presentation" in the work *On the Soul*. Without a presentation, intellectual activity is impossible. There is a similar process in geometric demonstrations. For example, when we draw a triangle, we don't focus on its exact size, but we still draw it with a specific size. Likewise, when we use our intellect, even if we are thinking about something abstract like first principles, we still imagine it as having size or quantity, even though we aren't really thinking about its size. On the other hand, if we are thinking about something that is normally quantitative but not fixed in size, we still imagine it as having a specific size, and only later do we ignore that part. Why we can't use our intellect without also thinking about continuous things like time is another question. We understand size and movement using the same part of us that understands time (which is also the part that remembers). The presentation involved in this understanding is something that affects the "common sense" we all have. So, the way we understand things like size, movement, and time comes from the primary ability to perceive. Therefore, memory, even of intellectual things, involves some kind of presentation. This means memory belongs to the faculty of perception in a direct way, while it only belongs to the intellect indirectly.

This explains why not only humans and animals with opinions or intelligence, but also certain other animals, have memory. If memory were purely about intellect, many lower animals wouldn't have memory, and probably no mortal beings would have it. As things stand, not all animals have memory because not all can perceive time. Whenever someone remembers seeing, hearing, or learning something, they have to recognize that this happened before. And the idea of "before" and "after" is about time.

So, if we ask which part of the soul is responsible for memory, it's clear that it's the part responsible for "presentation." All things that can be presented to us through our senses are immediately objects of memory, while things that involve the intellect are remembered indirectly, only through presentation.

One might wonder how it's possible to remember something that isn't there, especially since the experience (or presentation) itself is happening in the present. This is because we have to think of the memory as something like a picture. When we perceive something, it makes an impression on our minds, like a seal stamping an image onto wax. This is why people who are very emotional or are at a certain stage in life may not form memories, just as a seal wouldn't leave an impression on running water. In some people, the surface that receives the impression may be too worn out, like an old wall, or too hard, so the impression doesn't form at all. This is why very young and very old people have trouble with memory—they are either growing too fast or decaying. Similarly, people who think too fast or too slow have bad memories. The fast ones are too soft, so the impression doesn't last, while the slow ones are too hard, so no impression is made.

But if this is how memory works, we might wonder: when someone remembers something, are they remembering the impression itself, or are they remembering the thing the impression represents? If it's the impression, then it seems we wouldn't remember anything that isn't present. But if it's the thing itself, how can we remember something that isn't there, since we are only perceiving the impression? Even if we accept that there is something like a picture or an impression inside us, why does seeing this picture count as remembering the original thing and not just the picture itself? When someone remembers, they are focusing on the impression. So how do they remember something that isn't there, like they are seeing or hearing something that's not present?

The answer is that this kind of experience actually makes sense and does happen. Think of a painting on a panel—it is both a painting and a likeness. Even though it's one thing, it can be seen in two ways: as just a painting or as a likeness of something else. In the same way, the memory we hold inside us can be seen just as it is, or it can be seen as a representation of something else. When we focus on it by itself, it's just an image or a presentation, but when we see it as related to something else, it becomes a memory of that thing. When the memory is brought into our mind, if we focus on it as it is, we just have a thought. But if we think of it as being connected to something else, like a painting of a person we've never seen before, and we think of it as being a likeness of that person, then we are having a different experience. In the case of memory, one object in the mind is simply a thought, but the other is a memory because it's seen as a likeness of something else.

This explains why sometimes, when we have a certain thought or image in our minds, we aren't sure whether it's a memory or not. We might doubt whether we actually had the experience. But then, suddenly, we might get the idea that we've seen or heard this before. This happens when we shift our view from just thinking of the image by itself to thinking of it as connected to something else.

The opposite also happens, like in the case of people who are confused, like Antipheron of Oreus and others who suffer from mental disorders. They treat their random thoughts as if they were memories of things that actually happened. This happens when someone sees something that isn't really a likeness but treats it as if it is.

Mnemonic exercises, or memory exercises, are about helping someone remember something by constantly reminding them of it. This means looking at something repeatedly as a likeness, not just as a disconnected image.

So, we have now explained what memory is: it is a state where a presentation acts like a likeness of something else. As for which part of us is responsible for memory, we've shown that it is the part of our perception that also helps us understand time.

Next, we talk about recollection, and to explain it, we need to build on what we already discussed earlier. Recollection is not the same as gaining or recovering a memory. When someone first learns something, whether it's a scientific fact or something they've seen or experienced, they don't immediately recover a memory. That's because no memory has been formed before that moment, nor do they gain one from the start. It's only when this experience or knowledge becomes embedded in the soul that memory is formed. Therefore, memory doesn't happen at the same time the experience is happening.

Further, at the moment when the sensory experience or knowledge is fully embedded, a memory is established in the person who experienced it. This may involve sensory experiences or knowledge, which can sometimes be called scientific knowledge. One may remember, in an indirect way, certain things that are known scientifically. But remembering something, in the strict sense, only happens after time has passed. We remember things that we saw or experienced in the past; the moment of the original experience and the moment of remembering it are never the same.

Also, even after time has passed and one can be said to have a memory, that doesn't necessarily mean it's recollection. It's possible to remember something without actively trying to recollect it, just as a continued result of the original experience. But when someone retrieves a piece of knowledge or a memory after having forgotten it for a while, this retrieval is recollection. Remembering doesn't always mean you're recollecting, but recollecting always involves remembering, and the memory comes after successfully recollecting.

However, the idea that recollection means bringing back something that was once in your mind but was lost needs to be looked at more closely. This might be true, but it can also be false. For example, someone might learn the same thing twice from a teacher or discover it twice on their own. So, recollection should be defined differently from these acts; it must include something additional in the person who recollects, something beyond what they had when they first learned the information.

Recollection happens because one movement in the mind naturally leads to another. When these movements follow a necessary order, whenever the first movement happens, the second one will follow. If the order isn't necessary but just common, the second movement will follow most of the time. Some movements, after just one experience, leave a deeper impression than others do after many experiences. That's why some things, which we see or experience just once, are remembered better than others that we've seen many times.

So, when we are recollecting, we go through a series of earlier movements until we finally get to the one we are trying to remember. This explains why, when we try to remember, we search through thoughts, starting either from something we're currently thinking about or from something similar, opposite, or connected to what we're trying to remember. This is how recollection works: the movements we start with either match, happen at the same time, or form part of the movements of the idea we're trying to recall. So, the part we need to remember next is smaller and easier to reach.

That's how people go about recollecting, and it's also why we can sometimes recollect without even trying. The movement needed for recollection sometimes just comes after a different movement that set the stage for it. Usually, it's only after the earlier movements are triggered that the one needed for recollection follows. We don't need to trace a long chain of events to see how recollection works; even a short series will show the same process. It's clear that the method is the same in every case: one goes through a series of ideas, without having already searched for it or remembered it beforehand. Besides the natural order of experiences, there's also a customary order, and through habit, one movement often follows another in a predictable way.

So, when someone wants to recollect something, they start with a movement that will lead to the movement they want to recall. This is why attempts at recollection work best when they begin from the right starting point. The movements of memory follow one another in the same order as the original events. That's why things arranged in a fixed order, like steps in a geometric proof, are easier to remember, while things that are badly arranged are harder to remember.

Recollecting is also different from relearning in another way: when you recollect, you can, on your own, move from the first point to the next. If you can't do this without help from the outside, then you don't remember, and of course, you can't recollect. It often happens that even when someone can't recollect right away, they eventually succeed after trying. They do this by setting off many mental movements until they finally hit on one that leads to the memory they're seeking. Remembering (which is a requirement for recollecting) involves having a movement in the mind that can trigger the desired recollection. As we've said, this happens when the movements come from within the person.

But you have to find a starting point first. This is why people sometimes use memory tricks to help them recollect. They quickly move from one thought to another, like from milk to the color white, from white to mist, and from mist to moisture, which helps them remember autumn if that's what they were trying to recollect.

In general, starting from the middle of a series of events is often a good way to help you recollect any of them. If you don't remember before reaching the middle point, you might do so once you get there, or if not, nothing will help you. For example, if you're trying to recall a series of symbols like A, B, G, D, E, Z, I, H, O, and you don't remember what you want at E, you might remember O because from E, you could go toward D or Z. But if you're not searching for D or Z, then you might remember what you're looking for when you reach G if you were looking for H or I. But if it's none of these, you could try going back to A, and this process will apply to any series where you start from the middle. The reason you sometimes recollect and sometimes don't, even from the same starting point, is because there are different paths your mind can take, like from G to I or from G to D. If your mind doesn't take the same path as before, it will tend to follow the most familiar one. That's why we recollect things more quickly when we think about them often. Repetition makes the order feel more natural, and the more often we follow this path, the more like second nature it becomes.

However, in nature, things sometimes happen by chance or against the usual pattern, and this is even more common when habit is involved because habit doesn't follow natural law as strictly. This explains why, starting from the same point, our minds sometimes take the correct path and other times take a different one. This is especially true when something distracts the mind and pulls it off course. This also explains why, when we're trying to remember a name, we might recall a similar name but still get it wrong.

So, this is how recollection works. But the most important thing is that, for recollection to happen, we must recognize the time relationship of the thing we're trying to recollect. It's a fact that we have a way of distinguishing between longer and shorter times, similar to how we tell the difference between large and small spaces. It's not like some say, that our mind stretches out to the objects, like how they think our eyes send out rays to see things. Instead, we understand them through a proportional mental movement. Our minds hold similar forms and movements to the objects and events we've experienced, so thinking of larger or smaller objects happens in the same way. Therefore, just as we have forms in our minds that are proportional to the size of things, we also have something in our minds that is proportional to the time it took to experience them. Just like when you have movements in your mind between two points, you can recreate the original event in your mind.

Why, then, does the mind recall one thing rather than another? It's because the movement in the mind matches the proportions of what we're trying to remember. If the mental movement matches the event and the time, then we remember. If we only have one of these, then we don't.

There are two types of time-related movements in memory. Sometimes, when we remember a fact, we don't have a specific sense of the time it happened, like remembering we did something two days ago. Other times, we do have a clear sense of when it happened. Even when we don't clearly remember the time, we are still genuinely remembering. People often say they remember something but don't know exactly when it happened. This happens when they can't determine the length of time that passed.

People who have a good memory aren't necessarily the same people who are quick at recollecting. Recollection is different from remembering, not only in terms of time but also in that many animals can remember, but none that we know of, except humans, can recollect. The reason is that recollection is a kind of reasoning. Someone trying to recollect something concludes that they must have seen, heard, or experienced it before, and this process is like an investigation. Investigating in this way is something only animals with the ability to reason can do.

That recollection is connected to the body is proven by the fact that, when some people try hard to recollect but fail, the effort makes them uncomfortable. This discomfort persists even after they stop trying to recollect, especially in people who are melancholic. These people are particularly affected by things they imagine. The reason recollection isn't entirely under our control is similar to why someone who throws a stone can't stop it after it's been thrown. Once you start trying to recollect something, you set a process in motion in a physical part of the body where the memory resides. Those with moisture around the part of the body that controls perception feel the most discomfort from this. Once the moisture is set in motion, it's not easily calmed until the memory is found, and the process is complete. That's why feelings like anger or fear, once triggered, don't go away immediately, even if the person tries to calm themselves down. The emotions keep pushing forward, just like how someone might struggle to stop saying a word or humming a tune that's stuck in their head.

People with large upper bodies, like dwarfs, tend to have weaker memories compared to those with smaller upper bodies. This is because the extra weight presses down on the organ of perception, and their memory movements are scattered and unable to stay on track. These movements also struggle to find a direct path when trying to recollect. Children and elderly people also have weaker memories because there is too much movement in their bodies. The elderly are breaking down, and the young are still growing. Additionally, young children are physically similar to dwarfs.

This is our theory about memory and how remembering works. It explains the part of the soul that animals use to remember and how recollection happens, its definition, and the causes behind it.

• • •

The End

Thank you for Reading

Dear Reader,

We hope this timeless classic has sparked your imagination and enriched your literary journey. Now that you've turned the final page, we want to share a vision for the future of reading—one where every classic you've ever wanted to explore is at your fingertips, in a format that best suits your life.

We'd like to invite you to **gain immediate, unlimited digital & audiobook access** to hundreds of the most treasured literary classics ever written—along with the option to **secure deluxe paperback, hardcover & box set editions at printing cost**. Together, we can **spark a new global literary renaissance** alongside our small, independent publishing house called "The Library of Alexandria."

Thousands of years ago, the Library of Alexandria stood as a beacon of knowledge—until it was lost to history. We aim to reignite that spirit of preservation and discovery right now, in the modern age—only this time, it's accessible to all, in every language and every format.

Picture a world where every timeless classic, novel, poem, or philosophical treatise is not only available to read but also updated for today's readers—modernized, translated into any language or dialect, and ready to enjoy in any format you choose, whether that is in an eBook, audiobook, paperback, or deluxe hardcover & box set version a printing cost.

By joining our movement to **rebuild the modern Library of Alexandria**, you become part of an unprecedented mission to offer:

- **Unlimited Audiobook & eBook Access to the Greatest Classics of All Time**

  Instantly explore thousands of legendary works, from Plato and Shakespeare to Jane Austen and Leo Tolstoy. All are instantly ready to read or listen to, giving you a complete literary universe at your fingertips.

- **Paperback & Deluxe Editions at Printing Costs:**

  Purchase any title in a paperback, deluxe hardbound, or deluxe boxset edition at printing costs, shipped right to your doorstep. Curate your personal library of Alexandria with editions worthy of display—crafted to last, designed to captivate, and delivered straight to your door.

- **Modern translations for Contemporary Readers in all languages and dialects**

Discover a vast selection of classics reimagined in clear, current language—no more struggling with outdated phrases or obscure references. Next to the original versions, we aim to offer translations in as many languages and dialects as possible.

As we continue our translation efforts and add new languages, readers everywhere can connect with these works as if they were written today. *By bridging linguistic divides, you're contributing to ensuring that these timeless stories become more meaningful, accessible, and inspiring for people across the globe.*

- **Your Personal Library of Alexandria:**

Over the months and years, you'll curate a unique physical archive of classics—each volume a testament to your taste, curiosity, and love of knowledge. It's not just about owning books—it's about curating a cultural legacy you'll cherish and pass down for generations to come.

- **Join a Global Literary Renaissance:**

Your support fuels an ongoing mission: allowing us to reinvest in offering deluxe print editions (including special boxsets) at their true cost, broaden the range of available formats and translations, and extend the reach of these works to new audiences worldwide.

By joining today, you're not just preserving a legacy of masterpieces; *you set in motion a powerful wave of literary accessibility.*

We are more than a publisher—we're a movement, and we can't do it alone. Your support lets us scale our mission, preserving and reimagining history's greatest works for tomorrow's readers.

Become a Torchbearer of knowledge.

Thank you for picking up this book and allowing us into your literary journey. As you turn the pages, know that you're part of something larger: a global effort to keep these stories alive, share their wisdom across borders and generations, and spark a true cultural revival for the modern era.

If this resonates with you—please consider taking the next step. By visiting:
www.libraryofalexandria.com

With gratitude and a shared love of knowledge,

The Modern Library of Alexandria Team

Visit:

www.libraryofalexandria.com

Or scan the code below:

www.ingramcontent.com/pod-product-compliance
Lightning Source LLC
Chambersburg PA
CBHW012012290326
41934CB00017BA/3471